THIS BOOK BELONGS TO:

CONTACT INFORMATION	
NAME:	
ADDRESS:	
PHONE:	

START / END DATES

_____ / / _____   TO   _____ / / _____

DEDICATION

This Insect Journal is dedicated to all the people out there who love to hunt or collect bugs and insects and document their findings in the process.

You are my inspiration for producing books and I'm honored to be a part of keeping all of your insect and bug notes and records organized.

This journal notebook will help you record your details about your insects and bugs.

Thoughtfully put together with these sections to record: Weather, Where Did You Find It, Color, Number of Legs, Sound It Makes, Notes & Photo or Drawing.

HOW TO USE THIS BOOK

The purpose of this book is to keep all of your Insect & Bug notes all in one place. It will help keep you organized.

This Insect Journal will allow you to accurately document every detail about your insects & bugs.

Here are examples of the prompts for you to fill in and write about your experience in this book:

1. Date, Time & Season

2. Weather Conditions

3. Where Did You Find It?

4. Color of the Bug

5. Number of Legs

6. Sound It Makes

7. Notes

8. Photo or Drawing

BUG JOURNAL

DATE:		TIME:		SEASON:	○ SPRING ○ SUMMER ○ FALL ○ WINTER

WEATHER CONDITIONS:	○ HOT ○ WARM ○ SUNNY ○ CLOUDY ○ RAINY ○ WINDY ○ FOGGY ○ COLD
BUG NAME:	
WHERE DID YOU FIND IT?	
WHAT COLOR(S) IS THE BUG?	

NUMBER OF LEGS?		DOES IT HAVE WINGS?	○ YES ○ NO ○ NOT SURE
NUMBER OF LEGS?			

THE BUG IS...	○ BIG ○ SHINY ○ FAST ○ SCARY ○ LITTLE ○ SLOW ○ CUTE ○ ROUND ○ THIN

DOES IT MAKE ANY SOUND?	○ YES ○ NO	WAS IT ALONE OR IN A GROUP?	○ ALONE ○ GROUP

NOTES

PHOTO/DRAWING

BUG JOURNAL

DATE:		TIME:		SEASON:	○ SPRING ○ SUMMER ○ FALL ○ WINTER		
WEATHER CONDITIONS:		○ HOT ○ WARM ○ SUNNY ○ CLOUDY ○ RAINY ○ WINDY ○ FOGGY ○ COLD					
BUG NAME:							
WHERE DID YOU FIND IT?							
WHAT COLOR(S) IS THE BUG?							
NUMBER OF LEGS?			DOES IT HAVE WINGS?		○ YES ○ NO ○ NOT SURE		
NUMBER OF LEGS?							
THE BUG IS...		○ BIG ○ SHINY ○ FAST ○ SCARY ○ LITTLE ○ SLOW ○ CUTE ○ ROUND ○ THIN					
DOES IT MAKE ANY SOUND?		○ YES ○ NO	WAS IT ALONE OR IN A GROUP?		○ ALONE ○ GROUP		

NOTES

PHOTO/DRAWING

BUG JOURNAL

DATE:		TIME:		SEASON:	○ SPRING ○ SUMMER ○ FALL ○ WINTER
WEATHER CONDITIONS:		○ HOT ○ WARM ○ SUNNY ○ CLOUDY ○ RAINY ○ WINDY ○ FOGGY ○ COLD			
BUG NAME:					
WHERE DID YOU FIND IT?					
WHAT COLOR(S) IS THE BUG?					
NUMBER OF LEGS?		**DOES IT HAVE WINGS?**	○ YES ○ NO ○ NOT SURE		
NUMBER OF LEGS?					
THE BUG IS...		○ BIG ○ SHINY ○ FAST ○ SCARY ○ LITTLE ○ SLOW ○ CUTE ○ ROUND ○ THIN			
DOES IT MAKE ANY SOUND?	○ YES ○ NO	**WAS IT ALONE OR IN A GROUP?**	○ ALONE ○ GROUP		

NOTES

PHOTO/DRAWING

BUG JOURNAL

DATE:		TIME:		SEASON:	○ SPRING ○ SUMMER ○ FALL ○ WINTER	
WEATHER CONDITIONS:		○ HOT ○ WARM ○ SUNNY ○ CLOUDY ○ RAINY ○ WINDY ○ FOGGY ○ COLD				
BUG NAME:						
WHERE DID YOU FIND IT?						
WHAT COLOR(S) IS THE BUG?						
NUMBER OF LEGS?		DOES IT HAVE WINGS?		○ YES ○ NO ○ NOT SURE		
NUMBER OF LEGS?						
THE BUG IS...		○ BIG ○ SHINY ○ FAST ○ SCARY ○ LITTLE ○ SLOW ○ CUTE ○ ROUND ○ THIN				
DOES IT MAKE ANY SOUND?		○ YES ○ NO	WAS IT ALONE OR IN A GROUP?		○ ALONE ○ GROUP	

NOTES

PHOTO/DRAWING

BUG JOURNAL

DATE:		TIME:		SEASON:	○ SPRING ○ SUMMER ○ FALL ○ WINTER
WEATHER CONDITIONS:		○ HOT ○ WARM ○ SUNNY ○ CLOUDY ○ RAINY ○ WINDY ○ FOGGY ○ COLD			
BUG NAME:					
WHERE DID YOU FIND IT?					
WHAT COLOR(S) IS THE BUG?					
NUMBER OF LEGS?		**DOES IT HAVE WINGS?**	○ YES ○ NO ○ NOT SURE		
NUMBER OF LEGS?					
THE BUG IS...		○ BIG ○ SHINY ○ FAST ○ SCARY ○ LITTLE ○ SLOW ○ CUTE ○ ROUND ○ THIN			
DOES IT MAKE ANY SOUND?	○ YES ○ NO	**WAS IT ALONE OR IN A GROUP?**	○ ALONE ○ GROUP		

NOTES

PHOTO/DRAWING

BUG JOURNAL

DATE:		TIME:		SEASON:	○ SPRING ○ SUMMER ○ FALL ○ WINTER
WEATHER CONDITIONS:		○ HOT ○ WARM ○ SUNNY ○ CLOUDY ○ RAINY ○ WINDY ○ FOGGY ○ COLD			
BUG NAME:					
WHERE DID YOU FIND IT?					
WHAT COLOR(S) IS THE BUG?					
NUMBER OF LEGS?		DOES IT HAVE WINGS?	○ YES ○ NO ○ NOT SURE		
NUMBER OF LEGS?					
THE BUG IS...		○ BIG ○ SHINY ○ FAST ○ SCARY ○ LITTLE ○ SLOW ○ CUTE ○ ROUND ○ THIN			
DOES IT MAKE ANY SOUND?	○ YES ○ NO	WAS IT ALONE OR IN A GROUP?	○ ALONE ○ GROUP		

NOTES

PHOTO/DRAWING

BUG JOURNAL

DATE:		TIME:		SEASON:	○ SPRING ○ SUMMER ○ FALL ○ WINTER
WEATHER CONDITIONS:					○ HOT ○ WARM ○ SUNNY ○ CLOUDY ○ RAINY ○ WINDY ○ FOGGY ○ COLD
BUG NAME:					
WHERE DID YOU FIND IT?					
WHAT COLOR(S) IS THE BUG?					
NUMBER OF LEGS?			DOES IT HAVE WINGS?		○ YES ○ NO ○ NOT SURE
NUMBER OF LEGS?					
THE BUG IS...					○ BIG ○ SHINY ○ FAST ○ SCARY ○ LITTLE ○ SLOW ○ CUTE ○ ROUND ○ THIN
DOES IT MAKE ANY SOUND?		○ YES ○ NO	WAS IT ALONE OR IN A GROUP?		○ ALONE ○ GROUP

NOTES

PHOTO/DRAWING

BUG JOURNAL

DATE:		TIME:		SEASON:	○ SPRING ○ SUMMER ○ FALL ○ WINTER		
WEATHER CONDITIONS:		○ HOT ○ WARM ○ SUNNY ○ CLOUDY ○ RAINY ○ WINDY ○ FOGGY ○ COLD					
BUG NAME:							
WHERE DID YOU FIND IT?							
WHAT COLOR(S) IS THE BUG?							
NUMBER OF LEGS?		DOES IT HAVE WINGS?	○ YES ○ NO ○ NOT SURE				
NUMBER OF LEGS?							
THE BUG IS...	○ BIG ○ SHINY ○ FAST ○ SCARY ○ LITTLE ○ SLOW ○ CUTE ○ ROUND ○ THIN						
DOES IT MAKE ANY SOUND?	○ YES ○ NO	WAS IT ALONE OR IN A GROUP?	○ ALONE ○ GROUP				

NOTES

PHOTO/DRAWING

BUG JOURNAL

DATE:		TIME:		SEASON:	○ SPRING ○ SUMMER ○ FALL ○ WINTER		
WEATHER CONDITIONS:		○ HOT ○ WARM ○ SUNNY ○ CLOUDY ○ RAINY ○ WINDY ○ FOGGY ○ COLD					
BUG NAME:							
WHERE DID YOU FIND IT?							
WHAT COLOR(S) IS THE BUG?							
NUMBER OF LEGS?			**DOES IT HAVE WINGS?**	○ YES ○ NO ○ NOT SURE			
NUMBER OF LEGS?							
THE BUG IS...		○ BIG ○ SHINY ○ FAST ○ SCARY ○ LITTLE ○ SLOW ○ CUTE ○ ROUND ○ THIN					
DOES IT MAKE ANY SOUND?		○ YES ○ NO	**WAS IT ALONE OR IN A GROUP?**		○ ALONE ○ GROUP		

NOTES

PHOTO/DRAWING

BUG JOURNAL

DATE:		TIME:		SEASON:	○ SPRING ○ SUMMER ○ FALL ○ WINTER
WEATHER CONDITIONS:		○ HOT ○ WARM ○ SUNNY ○ CLOUDY ○ RAINY ○ WINDY ○ FOGGY ○ COLD			
BUG NAME:					
WHERE DID YOU FIND IT?					
WHAT COLOR(S) IS THE BUG?					
NUMBER OF LEGS?		DOES IT HAVE WINGS?	○ YES ○ NO ○ NOT SURE		
NUMBER OF LEGS?					
THE BUG IS...		○ BIG ○ SHINY ○ FAST ○ SCARY ○ LITTLE ○ SLOW ○ CUTE ○ ROUND ○ THIN			
DOES IT MAKE ANY SOUND?	○ YES ○ NO	WAS IT ALONE OR IN A GROUP?	○ ALONE ○ GROUP		

NOTES

PHOTO/DRAWING

BUG JOURNAL

DATE:		TIME:		SEASON:	○ SPRING ○ SUMMER ○ FALL ○ WINTER

WEATHER CONDITIONS:	○ HOT ○ WARM ○ SUNNY ○ CLOUDY ○ RAINY ○ WINDY ○ FOGGY ○ COLD
BUG NAME:	
WHERE DID YOU FIND IT?	
WHAT COLOR(S) IS THE BUG?	

NUMBER OF LEGS?		DOES IT HAVE WINGS?	○ YES ○ NO ○ NOT SURE

NUMBER OF LEGS?	
THE BUG IS...	○ BIG ○ SHINY ○ FAST ○ SCARY ○ LITTLE ○ SLOW ○ CUTE ○ ROUND ○ THIN

DOES IT MAKE ANY SOUND?	○ YES ○ NO	WAS IT ALONE OR IN A GROUP?	○ ALONE ○ GROUP

NOTES

PHOTO/DRAWING

BUG JOURNAL

DATE:		TIME:		SEASON:	○ SPRING ○ SUMMER ○ FALL ○ WINTER
WEATHER CONDITIONS:					○ HOT ○ WARM ○ SUNNY ○ CLOUDY ○ RAINY ○ WINDY ○ FOGGY ○ COLD
BUG NAME:					
WHERE DID YOU FIND IT?					
WHAT COLOR(S) IS THE BUG?					
NUMBER OF LEGS?		DOES IT HAVE WINGS?		○ YES ○ NO ○ NOT SURE	
NUMBER OF LEGS?					
THE BUG IS...		○ BIG ○ SHINY ○ FAST ○ SCARY ○ LITTLE ○ SLOW ○ CUTE ○ ROUND ○ THIN			
DOES IT MAKE ANY SOUND?		○ YES ○ NO	WAS IT ALONE OR IN A GROUP?		○ ALONE ○ GROUP

NOTES

PHOTO/DRAWING

BUG JOURNAL

DATE:		TIME:		SEASON:	○ SPRING ○ SUMMER ○ FALL ○ WINTER
WEATHER CONDITIONS:		○ HOT ○ WARM ○ SUNNY ○ CLOUDY ○ RAINY ○ WINDY ○ FOGGY ○ COLD			
BUG NAME:					
WHERE DID YOU FIND IT?					
WHAT COLOR(S) IS THE BUG?					
NUMBER OF LEGS?		**DOES IT HAVE WINGS?**	○ YES ○ NO ○ NOT SURE		
NUMBER OF LEGS?					
THE BUG IS...		○ BIG ○ SHINY ○ FAST ○ SCARY ○ LITTLE ○ SLOW ○ CUTE ○ ROUND ○ THIN			
DOES IT MAKE ANY SOUND?	○ YES ○ NO	**WAS IT ALONE OR IN A GROUP?**	○ ALONE ○ GROUP		

NOTES

PHOTO/DRAWING

BUG JOURNAL

DATE:		TIME:		SEASON:	○ SPRING ○ SUMMER ○ FALL ○ WINTER
WEATHER CONDITIONS:		○ HOT ○ WARM ○ SUNNY ○ CLOUDY ○ RAINY ○ WINDY ○ FOGGY ○ COLD			
BUG NAME:					
WHERE DID YOU FIND IT?					
WHAT COLOR(S) IS THE BUG?					
NUMBER OF LEGS?		**DOES IT HAVE WINGS?**	○ YES ○ NO ○ NOT SURE		
NUMBER OF LEGS?					
THE BUG IS...		○ BIG ○ SHINY ○ FAST ○ SCARY ○ LITTLE ○ SLOW ○ CUTE ○ ROUND ○ THIN			
DOES IT MAKE ANY SOUND?	○ YES ○ NO	**WAS IT ALONE OR IN A GROUP?**	○ ALONE ○ GROUP		

NOTES

PHOTO/DRAWING

BUG JOURNAL

DATE:		TIME:		SEASON:	○ SPRING ○ SUMMER ○ FALL ○ WINTER
WEATHER CONDITIONS:		○ HOT ○ WARM ○ SUNNY ○ CLOUDY ○ RAINY ○ WINDY ○ FOGGY ○ COLD			
BUG NAME:					
WHERE DID YOU FIND IT?					
WHAT COLOR(S) IS THE BUG?					
NUMBER OF LEGS?		DOES IT HAVE WINGS?	○ YES ○ NO ○ NOT SURE		
NUMBER OF LEGS?					
THE BUG IS...		○ BIG ○ SHINY ○ FAST ○ SCARY ○ LITTLE ○ SLOW ○ CUTE ○ ROUND ○ THIN			
DOES IT MAKE ANY SOUND?	○ YES ○ NO	WAS IT ALONE OR IN A GROUP?	○ ALONE ○ GROUP		

NOTES

PHOTO/DRAWING

BUG JOURNAL

DATE:		TIME:		SEASON:	○ SPRING ○ SUMMER ○ FALL ○ WINTER		
WEATHER CONDITIONS:	○ HOT ○ WARM ○ SUNNY ○ CLOUDY ○ RAINY ○ WINDY ○ FOGGY ○ COLD						
BUG NAME:							
WHERE DID YOU FIND IT?							
WHAT COLOR(S) IS THE BUG?							
NUMBER OF LEGS?		DOES IT HAVE WINGS?	○ YES ○ NO ○ NOT SURE				
NUMBER OF LEGS?							
THE BUG IS...	○ BIG ○ SHINY ○ FAST ○ SCARY ○ LITTLE ○ SLOW ○ CUTE ○ ROUND ○ THIN						
DOES IT MAKE ANY SOUND?	○ YES ○ NO	WAS IT ALONE OR IN A GROUP?	○ ALONE ○ GROUP				

NOTES

PHOTO/DRAWING

BUG JOURNAL

DATE:		TIME:		SEASON:	○ SPRING ○ SUMMER ○ FALL ○ WINTER

WEATHER CONDITIONS:	○ HOT ○ WARM ○ SUNNY ○ CLOUDY ○ RAINY ○ WINDY ○ FOGGY ○ COLD
BUG NAME:	
WHERE DID YOU FIND IT?	
WHAT COLOR(S) IS THE BUG?	

NUMBER OF LEGS?		DOES IT HAVE WINGS?	○ YES ○ NO ○ NOT SURE

NUMBER OF LEGS?	
THE BUG IS...	○ BIG ○ SHINY ○ FAST ○ SCARY ○ LITTLE ○ SLOW ○ CUTE ○ ROUND ○ THIN

DOES IT MAKE ANY SOUND?	○ YES ○ NO	WAS IT ALONE OR IN A GROUP?	○ ALONE ○ GROUP

NOTES

PHOTO/DRAWING

BUG JOURNAL

DATE:		TIME:		SEASON:	○ SPRING ○ SUMMER ○ FALL ○ WINTER
WEATHER CONDITIONS:		○ HOT ○ WARM ○ SUNNY ○ CLOUDY ○ RAINY ○ WINDY ○ FOGGY ○ COLD			
BUG NAME:					
WHERE DID YOU FIND IT?					
WHAT COLOR(S) IS THE BUG?					
NUMBER OF LEGS?		**DOES IT HAVE WINGS?**	○ YES ○ NO ○ NOT SURE		
NUMBER OF LEGS?					
THE BUG IS...		○ BIG ○ SHINY ○ FAST ○ SCARY ○ LITTLE ○ SLOW ○ CUTE ○ ROUND ○ THIN			
DOES IT MAKE ANY SOUND?	○ YES ○ NO	**WAS IT ALONE OR IN A GROUP?**	○ ALONE ○ GROUP		

NOTES

PHOTO/DRAWING

BUG JOURNAL

DATE:		TIME:		SEASON:	○ SPRING ○ SUMMER ○ FALL ○ WINTER		
WEATHER CONDITIONS:		○ HOT ○ WARM ○ SUNNY ○ CLOUDY ○ RAINY ○ WINDY ○ FOGGY ○ COLD					
BUG NAME:							
WHERE DID YOU FIND IT?							
WHAT COLOR(S) IS THE BUG?							
NUMBER OF LEGS?			**DOES IT HAVE WINGS?**	○ YES ○ NO ○ NOT SURE			
NUMBER OF LEGS?							
THE BUG IS...		○ BIG ○ SHINY ○ FAST ○ SCARY ○ LITTLE ○ SLOW ○ CUTE ○ ROUND ○ THIN					
DOES IT MAKE ANY SOUND?	○ YES ○ NO		**WAS IT ALONE OR IN A GROUP?**	○ ALONE ○ GROUP			

NOTES

PHOTO/DRAWING

BUG JOURNAL

DATE:		TIME:		SEASON:	○ SPRING ○ SUMMER ○ FALL ○ WINTER
WEATHER CONDITIONS:		○ HOT ○ WARM ○ SUNNY ○ CLOUDY ○ RAINY ○ WINDY ○ FOGGY ○ COLD			
BUG NAME:					
WHERE DID YOU FIND IT?					
WHAT COLOR(S) IS THE BUG?					
NUMBER OF LEGS?		DOES IT HAVE WINGS?	○ YES ○ NO ○ NOT SURE		
NUMBER OF LEGS?					
THE BUG IS...		○ BIG ○ SHINY ○ FAST ○ SCARY ○ LITTLE ○ SLOW ○ CUTE ○ ROUND ○ THIN			
DOES IT MAKE ANY SOUND?	○ YES ○ NO	WAS IT ALONE OR IN A GROUP?	○ ALONE ○ GROUP		

NOTES

PHOTO/DRAWING

BUG JOURNAL

DATE:		TIME:		SEASON:	○ SPRING ○ SUMMER ○ FALL ○ WINTER
WEATHER CONDITIONS:		○ HOT ○ WARM ○ SUNNY ○ CLOUDY ○ RAINY ○ WINDY ○ FOGGY ○ COLD			
BUG NAME:					
WHERE DID YOU FIND IT?					
WHAT COLOR(S) IS THE BUG?					
NUMBER OF LEGS?		DOES IT HAVE WINGS?	○ YES ○ NO ○ NOT SURE		
NUMBER OF LEGS?					
THE BUG IS...		○ BIG ○ SHINY ○ FAST ○ SCARY ○ LITTLE ○ SLOW ○ CUTE ○ ROUND ○ THIN			
DOES IT MAKE ANY SOUND?	○ YES ○ NO	WAS IT ALONE OR IN A GROUP?	○ ALONE ○ GROUP		

NOTES

PHOTO/DRAWING

BUG JOURNAL

DATE:		TIME:		SEASON:	○ SPRING ○ SUMMER ○ FALL ○ WINTER

WEATHER CONDITIONS:	○ HOT ○ WARM ○ SUNNY ○ CLOUDY ○ RAINY ○ WINDY ○ FOGGY ○ COLD
BUG NAME:	
WHERE DID YOU FIND IT?	
WHAT COLOR(S) IS THE BUG?	

NUMBER OF LEGS?		DOES IT HAVE WINGS?	○ YES ○ NO ○ NOT SURE

NUMBER OF LEGS?	
THE BUG IS...	○ BIG ○ SHINY ○ FAST ○ SCARY ○ LITTLE ○ SLOW ○ CUTE ○ ROUND ○ THIN

DOES IT MAKE ANY SOUND?	○ YES ○ NO	WAS IT ALONE OR IN A GROUP?	○ ALONE ○ GROUP

NOTES

PHOTO/DRAWING

BUG JOURNAL

DATE:		TIME:		SEASON:	○ SPRING ○ SUMMER ○ FALL ○ WINTER
WEATHER CONDITIONS:		○ HOT ○ WARM ○ SUNNY ○ CLOUDY ○ RAINY ○ WINDY ○ FOGGY ○ COLD			
BUG NAME:					
WHERE DID YOU FIND IT?					
WHAT COLOR(S) IS THE BUG?					
NUMBER OF LEGS?		DOES IT HAVE WINGS?	○ YES ○ NO ○ NOT SURE		
NUMBER OF LEGS?					
THE BUG IS...		○ BIG ○ SHINY ○ FAST ○ SCARY ○ LITTLE ○ SLOW ○ CUTE ○ ROUND ○ THIN			
DOES IT MAKE ANY SOUND?	○ YES ○ NO	WAS IT ALONE OR IN A GROUP?	○ ALONE ○ GROUP		

NOTES

PHOTO/DRAWING

BUG JOURNAL

DATE:		TIME:		SEASON:	○ SPRING ○ SUMMER ○ FALL ○ WINTER		
WEATHER CONDITIONS:		○ HOT ○ WARM ○ SUNNY ○ CLOUDY ○ RAINY ○ WINDY ○ FOGGY ○ COLD					
BUG NAME:							
WHERE DID YOU FIND IT?							
WHAT COLOR(S) IS THE BUG?							
NUMBER OF LEGS?			**DOES IT HAVE WINGS?**	○ YES ○ NO ○ NOT SURE			
NUMBER OF LEGS?							
THE BUG IS...		○ BIG ○ SHINY ○ FAST ○ SCARY ○ LITTLE ○ SLOW ○ CUTE ○ ROUND ○ THIN					
DOES IT MAKE ANY SOUND?	○ YES ○ NO		**WAS IT ALONE OR IN A GROUP?**	○ ALONE ○ GROUP			

NOTES

PHOTO/DRAWING

BUG JOURNAL

DATE:		TIME:		SEASON:	○ SPRING ○ SUMMER ○ FALL ○ WINTER
WEATHER CONDITIONS:		○ HOT ○ WARM ○ SUNNY ○ CLOUDY ○ RAINY ○ WINDY ○ FOGGY ○ COLD			
BUG NAME:					
WHERE DID YOU FIND IT?					
WHAT COLOR(S) IS THE BUG?					
NUMBER OF LEGS?		DOES IT HAVE WINGS?	○ YES ○ NO ○ NOT SURE		
NUMBER OF LEGS?					
THE BUG IS...		○ BIG ○ SHINY ○ FAST ○ SCARY ○ LITTLE ○ SLOW ○ CUTE ○ ROUND ○ THIN			
DOES IT MAKE ANY SOUND?	○ YES ○ NO	WAS IT ALONE OR IN A GROUP?	○ ALONE ○ GROUP		

NOTES

PHOTO/DRAWING

BUG JOURNAL

DATE:		TIME:		SEASON:	○ SPRING ○ SUMMER ○ FALL ○ WINTER		
WEATHER CONDITIONS:		○ HOT ○ WARM ○ SUNNY ○ CLOUDY ○ RAINY ○ WINDY ○ FOGGY ○ COLD					
BUG NAME:							
WHERE DID YOU FIND IT?							
WHAT COLOR(S) IS THE BUG?							
NUMBER OF LEGS?		DOES IT HAVE WINGS?		○ YES ○ NO ○ NOT SURE			
NUMBER OF LEGS?							
THE BUG IS...		○ BIG ○ SHINY ○ FAST ○ SCARY ○ LITTLE ○ SLOW ○ CUTE ○ ROUND ○ THIN					
DOES IT MAKE ANY SOUND?	○ YES ○ NO	WAS IT ALONE OR IN A GROUP?		○ ALONE ○ GROUP			

NOTES

PHOTO/DRAWING

BUG JOURNAL

DATE:		TIME:		SEASON:	○ SPRING ○ SUMMER ○ FALL ○ WINTER
WEATHER CONDITIONS:					○ HOT ○ WARM ○ SUNNY ○ CLOUDY ○ RAINY ○ WINDY ○ FOGGY ○ COLD
BUG NAME:					
WHERE DID YOU FIND IT?					
WHAT COLOR(S) IS THE BUG?					
NUMBER OF LEGS?			DOES IT HAVE WINGS?		○ YES ○ NO ○ NOT SURE
NUMBER OF LEGS?					
THE BUG IS...					○ BIG ○ SHINY ○ FAST ○ SCARY ○ LITTLE ○ SLOW ○ CUTE ○ ROUND ○ THIN
DOES IT MAKE ANY SOUND?		○ YES ○ NO	WAS IT ALONE OR IN A GROUP?		○ ALONE ○ GROUP

NOTES

PHOTO/DRAWING

BUG JOURNAL

DATE:		TIME:		SEASON:	○ SPRING ○ SUMMER ○ FALL ○ WINTER
WEATHER CONDITIONS:		○ HOT ○ WARM ○ SUNNY ○ CLOUDY ○ RAINY ○ WINDY ○ FOGGY ○ COLD			
BUG NAME:					
WHERE DID YOU FIND IT?					
WHAT COLOR(S) IS THE BUG?					
NUMBER OF LEGS?		DOES IT HAVE WINGS?	○ YES ○ NO ○ NOT SURE		
NUMBER OF LEGS?					
THE BUG IS...		○ BIG ○ SHINY ○ FAST ○ SCARY ○ LITTLE ○ SLOW ○ CUTE ○ ROUND ○ THIN			
DOES IT MAKE ANY SOUND?	○ YES ○ NO	WAS IT ALONE OR IN A GROUP?	○ ALONE ○ GROUP		

NOTES

PHOTO/DRAWING

BUG JOURNAL

DATE:		TIME:		SEASON:	○ SPRING ○ SUMMER ○ FALL ○ WINTER
WEATHER CONDITIONS:		○ HOT ○ WARM ○ SUNNY ○ CLOUDY ○ RAINY ○ WINDY ○ FOGGY ○ COLD			
BUG NAME:					
WHERE DID YOU FIND IT?					
WHAT COLOR(S) IS THE BUG?					
NUMBER OF LEGS?		DOES IT HAVE WINGS?	○ YES ○ NO ○ NOT SURE		
NUMBER OF LEGS?					
THE BUG IS...		○ BIG ○ SHINY ○ FAST ○ SCARY ○ LITTLE ○ SLOW ○ CUTE ○ ROUND ○ THIN			
DOES IT MAKE ANY SOUND?	○ YES ○ NO	WAS IT ALONE OR IN A GROUP?	○ ALONE ○ GROUP		

NOTES

PHOTO/DRAWING

BUG JOURNAL

DATE:		TIME:		SEASON:	○ SPRING ○ SUMMER ○ FALL ○ WINTER
WEATHER CONDITIONS:		○ HOT ○ WARM ○ SUNNY ○ CLOUDY ○ RAINY ○ WINDY ○ FOGGY ○ COLD			
BUG NAME:					
WHERE DID YOU FIND IT?					
WHAT COLOR(S) IS THE BUG?					
NUMBER OF LEGS?		DOES IT HAVE WINGS?	○ YES ○ NO ○ NOT SURE		
NUMBER OF LEGS?					
THE BUG IS...		○ BIG ○ SHINY ○ FAST ○ SCARY ○ LITTLE ○ SLOW ○ CUTE ○ ROUND ○ THIN			
DOES IT MAKE ANY SOUND?	○ YES ○ NO	WAS IT ALONE OR IN A GROUP?	○ ALONE ○ GROUP		

NOTES

PHOTO/DRAWING

BUG JOURNAL

DATE:		TIME:		SEASON:	○ SPRING ○ SUMMER ○ FALL ○ WINTER

WEATHER CONDITIONS:	○ HOT ○ WARM ○ SUNNY ○ CLOUDY ○ RAINY ○ WINDY ○ FOGGY ○ COLD
BUG NAME:	
WHERE DID YOU FIND IT?	
WHAT COLOR(S) IS THE BUG?	

NUMBER OF LEGS?		DOES IT HAVE WINGS?	○ YES ○ NO ○ NOT SURE

NUMBER OF LEGS?	
THE BUG IS...	○ BIG ○ SHINY ○ FAST ○ SCARY ○ LITTLE ○ SLOW ○ CUTE ○ ROUND ○ THIN

DOES IT MAKE ANY SOUND?	○ YES ○ NO	WAS IT ALONE OR IN A GROUP?	○ ALONE ○ GROUP

NOTES

PHOTO/DRAWING

BUG JOURNAL

DATE:		TIME:		SEASON:	○ SPRING ○ SUMMER ○ FALL ○ WINTER
WEATHER CONDITIONS:		○ HOT ○ WARM ○ SUNNY ○ CLOUDY ○ RAINY ○ WINDY ○ FOGGY ○ COLD			
BUG NAME:					
WHERE DID YOU FIND IT?					
WHAT COLOR(S) IS THE BUG?					
NUMBER OF LEGS?		DOES IT HAVE WINGS?	○ YES ○ NO ○ NOT SURE		
NUMBER OF LEGS?					
THE BUG IS...		○ BIG ○ SHINY ○ FAST ○ SCARY ○ LITTLE ○ SLOW ○ CUTE ○ ROUND ○ THIN			
DOES IT MAKE ANY SOUND?	○ YES ○ NO	WAS IT ALONE OR IN A GROUP?	○ ALONE ○ GROUP		

NOTES

PHOTO/DRAWING

BUG JOURNAL

DATE:		TIME:		SEASON:	○ SPRING ○ SUMMER ○ FALL ○ WINTER
WEATHER CONDITIONS:					○ HOT ○ WARM ○ SUNNY ○ CLOUDY ○ RAINY ○ WINDY ○ FOGGY ○ COLD
BUG NAME:					
WHERE DID YOU FIND IT?					
WHAT COLOR(S) IS THE BUG?					
NUMBER OF LEGS?		DOES IT HAVE WINGS?			○ YES ○ NO ○ NOT SURE
NUMBER OF LEGS?					
THE BUG IS...		○ BIG ○ SHINY ○ FAST ○ SCARY ○ LITTLE ○ SLOW ○ CUTE ○ ROUND ○ THIN			
DOES IT MAKE ANY SOUND?	○ YES ○ NO	WAS IT ALONE OR IN A GROUP?			○ ALONE ○ GROUP

NOTES

PHOTO/DRAWING

BUG JOURNAL

DATE:		TIME:		SEASON:	○ SPRING ○ SUMMER ○ FALL ○ WINTER
WEATHER CONDITIONS:		○ HOT ○ WARM ○ SUNNY ○ CLOUDY ○ RAINY ○ WINDY ○ FOGGY ○ COLD			
BUG NAME:					
WHERE DID YOU FIND IT?					
WHAT COLOR(S) IS THE BUG?					
NUMBER OF LEGS?		**DOES IT HAVE WINGS?**	○ YES ○ NO ○ NOT SURE		
NUMBER OF LEGS?					
THE BUG IS...		○ BIG ○ SHINY ○ FAST ○ SCARY ○ LITTLE ○ SLOW ○ CUTE ○ ROUND ○ THIN			
DOES IT MAKE ANY SOUND?	○ YES ○ NO	**WAS IT ALONE OR IN A GROUP?**	○ ALONE ○ GROUP		

NOTES

PHOTO/DRAWING

BUG JOURNAL

DATE:		TIME:		SEASON:	○ SPRING ○ SUMMER ○ FALL ○ WINTER
WEATHER CONDITIONS:		○ HOT ○ WARM ○ SUNNY ○ CLOUDY ○ RAINY ○ WINDY ○ FOGGY ○ COLD			
BUG NAME:					
WHERE DID YOU FIND IT?					
WHAT COLOR(S) IS THE BUG?					
NUMBER OF LEGS?		DOES IT HAVE WINGS?	○ YES ○ NO ○ NOT SURE		
NUMBER OF LEGS?					
THE BUG IS...		○ BIG ○ SHINY ○ FAST ○ SCARY ○ LITTLE ○ SLOW ○ CUTE ○ ROUND ○ THIN			
DOES IT MAKE ANY SOUND?	○ YES ○ NO	WAS IT ALONE OR IN A GROUP?	○ ALONE ○ GROUP		

NOTES

PHOTO/DRAWING

BUG JOURNAL

DATE:		TIME:		SEASON:	○ SPRING ○ SUMMER ○ FALL ○ WINTER
WEATHER CONDITIONS:		○ HOT ○ WARM ○ SUNNY ○ CLOUDY ○ RAINY ○ WINDY ○ FOGGY ○ COLD			
BUG NAME:					
WHERE DID YOU FIND IT?					
WHAT COLOR(S) IS THE BUG?					
NUMBER OF LEGS?		**DOES IT HAVE WINGS?**	○ YES ○ NO ○ NOT SURE		
NUMBER OF LEGS?					
THE BUG IS...		○ BIG ○ SHINY ○ FAST ○ SCARY ○ LITTLE ○ SLOW ○ CUTE ○ ROUND ○ THIN			
DOES IT MAKE ANY SOUND?	○ YES ○ NO	**WAS IT ALONE OR IN A GROUP?**	○ ALONE ○ GROUP		

NOTES

PHOTO/DRAWING

BUG JOURNAL

DATE:		TIME:		SEASON:	○ SPRING ○ SUMMER ○ FALL ○ WINTER
WEATHER CONDITIONS:		○ HOT ○ WARM ○ SUNNY ○ CLOUDY ○ RAINY ○ WINDY ○ FOGGY ○ COLD			
BUG NAME:					
WHERE DID YOU FIND IT?					
WHAT COLOR(S) IS THE BUG?					
NUMBER OF LEGS?		DOES IT HAVE WINGS?	○ YES ○ NO ○ NOT SURE		
NUMBER OF LEGS?					
THE BUG IS...		○ BIG ○ SHINY ○ FAST ○ SCARY ○ LITTLE ○ SLOW ○ CUTE ○ ROUND ○ THIN			
DOES IT MAKE ANY SOUND?	○ YES ○ NO	WAS IT ALONE OR IN A GROUP?	○ ALONE ○ GROUP		

NOTES

PHOTO/DRAWING

BUG JOURNAL

DATE:		TIME:		SEASON:	○ SPRING ○ SUMMER ○ FALL ○ WINTER		
WEATHER CONDITIONS:		○ HOT ○ WARM ○ SUNNY ○ CLOUDY ○ RAINY ○ WINDY ○ FOGGY ○ COLD					
BUG NAME:							
WHERE DID YOU FIND IT?							
WHAT COLOR(S) IS THE BUG?							
NUMBER OF LEGS?			DOES IT HAVE WINGS?		○ YES ○ NO ○ NOT SURE		
NUMBER OF LEGS?							
THE BUG IS...		○ BIG ○ SHINY ○ FAST ○ SCARY ○ LITTLE ○ SLOW ○ CUTE ○ ROUND ○ THIN					
DOES IT MAKE ANY SOUND?	○ YES ○ NO		WAS IT ALONE OR IN A GROUP?		○ ALONE ○ GROUP		

NOTES

PHOTO/DRAWING

BUG JOURNAL

DATE:		TIME:		SEASON:	○ SPRING ○ SUMMER ○ FALL ○ WINTER
WEATHER CONDITIONS:		○ HOT ○ WARM ○ SUNNY ○ CLOUDY ○ RAINY ○ WINDY ○ FOGGY ○ COLD			
BUG NAME:					
WHERE DID YOU FIND IT?					
WHAT COLOR(S) IS THE BUG?					
NUMBER OF LEGS?		DOES IT HAVE WINGS?	○ YES ○ NO ○ NOT SURE		
NUMBER OF LEGS?					
THE BUG IS...		○ BIG ○ SHINY ○ FAST ○ SCARY ○ LITTLE ○ SLOW ○ CUTE ○ ROUND ○ THIN			
DOES IT MAKE ANY SOUND?	○ YES ○ NO	WAS IT ALONE OR IN A GROUP?	○ ALONE ○ GROUP		

NOTES

PHOTO/DRAWING

BUG JOURNAL

DATE:		TIME:		SEASON:	○ SPRING ○ SUMMER ○ FALL ○ WINTER
WEATHER CONDITIONS:		○ HOT ○ WARM ○ SUNNY ○ CLOUDY ○ RAINY ○ WINDY ○ FOGGY ○ COLD			
BUG NAME:					
WHERE DID YOU FIND IT?					
WHAT COLOR(S) IS THE BUG?					
NUMBER OF LEGS?		DOES IT HAVE WINGS?	○ YES ○ NO ○ NOT SURE		
NUMBER OF LEGS?					
THE BUG IS...		○ BIG ○ SHINY ○ FAST ○ SCARY ○ LITTLE ○ SLOW ○ CUTE ○ ROUND ○ THIN			
DOES IT MAKE ANY SOUND?	○ YES ○ NO	WAS IT ALONE OR IN A GROUP?	○ ALONE ○ GROUP		

NOTES

PHOTO/DRAWING

BUG JOURNAL

DATE:		TIME:		SEASON:	○ SPRING ○ SUMMER ○ FALL ○ WINTER
WEATHER CONDITIONS:		○ HOT ○ WARM ○ SUNNY ○ CLOUDY ○ RAINY ○ WINDY ○ FOGGY ○ COLD			
BUG NAME:					
WHERE DID YOU FIND IT?					
WHAT COLOR(S) IS THE BUG?					
NUMBER OF LEGS?		**DOES IT HAVE WINGS?**	○ YES ○ NO ○ NOT SURE		
NUMBER OF LEGS?					
THE BUG IS...		○ BIG ○ SHINY ○ FAST ○ SCARY ○ LITTLE ○ SLOW ○ CUTE ○ ROUND ○ THIN			
DOES IT MAKE ANY SOUND?	○ YES ○ NO	**WAS IT ALONE OR IN A GROUP?**	○ ALONE ○ GROUP		

NOTES

PHOTO/DRAWING

BUG JOURNAL

DATE:		TIME:		SEASON:	○ SPRING ○ SUMMER ○ FALL ○ WINTER			
WEATHER CONDITIONS:		○ HOT ○ WARM ○ SUNNY ○ CLOUDY ○ RAINY ○ WINDY ○ FOGGY ○ COLD						
BUG NAME:								
WHERE DID YOU FIND IT?								
WHAT COLOR(S) IS THE BUG?								
NUMBER OF LEGS?			DOES IT HAVE WINGS?		○ YES ○ NO ○ NOT SURE			
NUMBER OF LEGS?								
THE BUG IS...		○ BIG ○ SHINY ○ FAST ○ SCARY ○ LITTLE ○ SLOW ○ CUTE ○ ROUND ○ THIN						
DOES IT MAKE ANY SOUND?		○ YES ○ NO	WAS IT ALONE OR IN A GROUP?		○ ALONE ○ GROUP			

NOTES

PHOTO/DRAWING

BUG JOURNAL

DATE:		TIME:		SEASON:	○ SPRING ○ SUMMER ○ FALL ○ WINTER
WEATHER CONDITIONS:					○ HOT ○ WARM ○ SUNNY ○ CLOUDY ○ RAINY ○ WINDY ○ FOGGY ○ COLD
BUG NAME:					
WHERE DID YOU FIND IT?					
WHAT COLOR(S) IS THE BUG?					
NUMBER OF LEGS?		DOES IT HAVE WINGS?		○ YES ○ NO ○ NOT SURE	
NUMBER OF LEGS?					
THE BUG IS...		○ BIG ○ SHINY ○ FAST ○ SCARY ○ LITTLE ○ SLOW ○ CUTE ○ ROUND ○ THIN			
DOES IT MAKE ANY SOUND?	○ YES ○ NO	WAS IT ALONE OR IN A GROUP?		○ ALONE ○ GROUP	

NOTES

PHOTO/DRAWING

BUG JOURNAL

DATE:		TIME:		SEASON:	○ SPRING ○ SUMMER ○ FALL ○ WINTER

WEATHER CONDITIONS:	○ HOT ○ WARM ○ SUNNY ○ CLOUDY ○ RAINY ○ WINDY ○ FOGGY ○ COLD
BUG NAME:	
WHERE DID YOU FIND IT?	
WHAT COLOR(S) IS THE BUG?	

NUMBER OF LEGS?		DOES IT HAVE WINGS?	○ YES ○ NO ○ NOT SURE

NUMBER OF LEGS?	
THE BUG IS...	○ BIG ○ SHINY ○ FAST ○ SCARY ○ LITTLE ○ SLOW ○ CUTE ○ ROUND ○ THIN

DOES IT MAKE ANY SOUND?	○ YES ○ NO	WAS IT ALONE OR IN A GROUP?	○ ALONE ○ GROUP

NOTES

PHOTO/DRAWING

BUG JOURNAL

DATE:		TIME:		SEASON:	○ SPRING ○ SUMMER ○ FALL ○ WINTER
WEATHER CONDITIONS:			○ HOT ○ WARM ○ SUNNY ○ CLOUDY ○ RAINY ○ WINDY ○ FOGGY ○ COLD		
BUG NAME:					
WHERE DID YOU FIND IT?					
WHAT COLOR(S) IS THE BUG?					
NUMBER OF LEGS?		DOES IT HAVE WINGS?	○ YES ○ NO ○ NOT SURE		
NUMBER OF LEGS?					
THE BUG IS...		○ BIG ○ SHINY ○ FAST ○ SCARY ○ LITTLE ○ SLOW ○ CUTE ○ ROUND ○ THIN			
DOES IT MAKE ANY SOUND?	○ YES ○ NO	WAS IT ALONE OR IN A GROUP?	○ ALONE ○ GROUP		

NOTES

PHOTO/DRAWING

BUG JOURNAL

DATE:		TIME:		SEASON:	○ SPRING ○ SUMMER ○ FALL ○ WINTER		
WEATHER CONDITIONS:		○ HOT ○ WARM ○ SUNNY ○ CLOUDY ○ RAINY ○ WINDY ○ FOGGY ○ COLD					
BUG NAME:							
WHERE DID YOU FIND IT?							
WHAT COLOR(S) IS THE BUG?							
NUMBER OF LEGS?			DOES IT HAVE WINGS?	○ YES ○ NO ○ NOT SURE			
NUMBER OF LEGS?							
THE BUG IS...		○ BIG ○ SHINY ○ FAST ○ SCARY ○ LITTLE ○ SLOW ○ CUTE ○ ROUND ○ THIN					
DOES IT MAKE ANY SOUND?		○ YES ○ NO	WAS IT ALONE OR IN A GROUP?		○ ALONE ○ GROUP		

NOTES

PHOTO/DRAWING

BUG JOURNAL

DATE:		TIME:		SEASON:	○ SPRING ○ SUMMER ○ FALL ○ WINTER
WEATHER CONDITIONS:		○ HOT ○ WARM ○ SUNNY ○ CLOUDY ○ RAINY ○ WINDY ○ FOGGY ○ COLD			
BUG NAME:					
WHERE DID YOU FIND IT?					
WHAT COLOR(S) IS THE BUG?					
NUMBER OF LEGS?		**DOES IT HAVE WINGS?**	○ YES ○ NO ○ NOT SURE		
NUMBER OF LEGS?					
THE BUG IS...		○ BIG ○ SHINY ○ FAST ○ SCARY ○ LITTLE ○ SLOW ○ CUTE ○ ROUND ○ THIN			
DOES IT MAKE ANY SOUND?	○ YES ○ NO	**WAS IT ALONE OR IN A GROUP?**	○ ALONE ○ GROUP		

NOTES

PHOTO/DRAWING

BUG JOURNAL

DATE:		TIME:		SEASON:	○ SPRING ○ SUMMER ○ FALL ○ WINTER
WEATHER CONDITIONS:					○ HOT ○ WARM ○ SUNNY ○ CLOUDY ○ RAINY ○ WINDY ○ FOGGY ○ COLD
BUG NAME:					
WHERE DID YOU FIND IT?					
WHAT COLOR(S) IS THE BUG?					
NUMBER OF LEGS?			DOES IT HAVE WINGS?	○ YES ○ NO ○ NOT SURE	
NUMBER OF LEGS?					
THE BUG IS...			○ BIG ○ SHINY ○ FAST ○ SCARY ○ LITTLE ○ SLOW ○ CUTE ○ ROUND ○ THIN		
DOES IT MAKE ANY SOUND?	○ YES ○ NO	WAS IT ALONE OR IN A GROUP?		○ ALONE ○ GROUP	

NOTES

PHOTO/DRAWING

BUG JOURNAL

DATE:		TIME:		SEASON:	○ SPRING ○ SUMMER ○ FALL ○ WINTER		
WEATHER CONDITIONS:		○ HOT ○ WARM ○ SUNNY ○ CLOUDY ○ RAINY ○ WINDY ○ FOGGY ○ COLD					
BUG NAME:							
WHERE DID YOU FIND IT?							
WHAT COLOR(S) IS THE BUG?							
NUMBER OF LEGS?		DOES IT HAVE WINGS?		○ YES ○ NO ○ NOT SURE			
NUMBER OF LEGS?							
THE BUG IS...		○ BIG ○ SHINY ○ FAST ○ SCARY ○ LITTLE ○ SLOW ○ CUTE ○ ROUND ○ THIN					
DOES IT MAKE ANY SOUND?		○ YES ○ NO	WAS IT ALONE OR IN A GROUP?		○ ALONE ○ GROUP		

NOTES

PHOTO/DRAWING

BUG JOURNAL

DATE:		TIME:		SEASON:	○ SPRING ○ SUMMER ○ FALL ○ WINTER
WEATHER CONDITIONS:		○ HOT ○ WARM ○ SUNNY ○ CLOUDY ○ RAINY ○ WINDY ○ FOGGY ○ COLD			
BUG NAME:					
WHERE DID YOU FIND IT?					
WHAT COLOR(S) IS THE BUG?					
NUMBER OF LEGS?		**DOES IT HAVE WINGS?**	○ YES ○ NO ○ NOT SURE		
NUMBER OF LEGS?					
THE BUG IS...		○ BIG ○ SHINY ○ FAST ○ SCARY ○ LITTLE ○ SLOW ○ CUTE ○ ROUND ○ THIN			
DOES IT MAKE ANY SOUND?	○ YES ○ NO	**WAS IT ALONE OR IN A GROUP?**	○ ALONE ○ GROUP		

NOTES

PHOTO/DRAWING

BUG JOURNAL

DATE:		TIME:		SEASON:	○ SPRING ○ SUMMER ○ FALL ○ WINTER

WEATHER CONDITIONS:	○ HOT ○ WARM ○ SUNNY ○ CLOUDY ○ RAINY ○ WINDY ○ FOGGY ○ COLD
BUG NAME:	
WHERE DID YOU FIND IT?	
WHAT COLOR(S) IS THE BUG?	

NUMBER OF LEGS?		DOES IT HAVE WINGS?	○ YES ○ NO ○ NOT SURE

NUMBER OF LEGS?	
THE BUG IS...	○ BIG ○ SHINY ○ FAST ○ SCARY ○ LITTLE ○ SLOW ○ CUTE ○ ROUND ○ THIN

DOES IT MAKE ANY SOUND?	○ YES ○ NO	WAS IT ALONE OR IN A GROUP?	○ ALONE ○ GROUP

NOTES

PHOTO/DRAWING

BUG JOURNAL

DATE:		TIME:		SEASON:	○ SPRING ○ SUMMER ○ FALL ○ WINTER
WEATHER CONDITIONS:		○ HOT ○ WARM ○ SUNNY ○ CLOUDY ○ RAINY ○ WINDY ○ FOGGY ○ COLD			
BUG NAME:					
WHERE DID YOU FIND IT?					
WHAT COLOR(S) IS THE BUG?					
NUMBER OF LEGS?		**DOES IT HAVE WINGS?**	○ YES ○ NO ○ NOT SURE		
NUMBER OF LEGS?					
THE BUG IS...		○ BIG ○ SHINY ○ FAST ○ SCARY ○ LITTLE ○ SLOW ○ CUTE ○ ROUND ○ THIN			
DOES IT MAKE ANY SOUND?	○ YES ○ NO	**WAS IT ALONE OR IN A GROUP?**	○ ALONE ○ GROUP		

NOTES

PHOTO/DRAWING

BUG JOURNAL

DATE:		TIME:		SEASON:	○ SPRING ○ SUMMER ○ FALL ○ WINTER
WEATHER CONDITIONS:					○ HOT ○ WARM ○ SUNNY ○ CLOUDY ○ RAINY ○ WINDY ○ FOGGY ○ COLD
BUG NAME:					
WHERE DID YOU FIND IT?					
WHAT COLOR(S) IS THE BUG?					
NUMBER OF LEGS?		**DOES IT HAVE WINGS?**	○ YES ○ NO ○ NOT SURE		
NUMBER OF LEGS?					
THE BUG IS...		○ BIG ○ SHINY ○ FAST ○ SCARY ○ LITTLE ○ SLOW ○ CUTE ○ ROUND ○ THIN			
DOES IT MAKE ANY SOUND?	○ YES ○ NO	**WAS IT ALONE OR IN A GROUP?**	○ ALONE ○ GROUP		

NOTES

PHOTO/DRAWING

BUG JOURNAL

DATE:		TIME:		SEASON:	○ SPRING ○ SUMMER ○ FALL ○ WINTER		
WEATHER CONDITIONS:		○ HOT ○ WARM ○ SUNNY ○ CLOUDY ○ RAINY ○ WINDY ○ FOGGY ○ COLD					
BUG NAME:							
WHERE DID YOU FIND IT?							
WHAT COLOR(S) IS THE BUG?							
NUMBER OF LEGS?			DOES IT HAVE WINGS?		○ YES ○ NO ○ NOT SURE		
NUMBER OF LEGS?							
THE BUG IS...		○ BIG ○ SHINY ○ FAST ○ SCARY ○ LITTLE ○ SLOW ○ CUTE ○ ROUND ○ THIN					
DOES IT MAKE ANY SOUND?	○ YES ○ NO		WAS IT ALONE OR IN A GROUP?		○ ALONE ○ GROUP		

NOTES

PHOTO/DRAWING

BUG JOURNAL

DATE:		TIME:		SEASON:	○ SPRING ○ SUMMER ○ FALL ○ WINTER
WEATHER CONDITIONS:		○ HOT ○ WARM ○ SUNNY ○ CLOUDY ○ RAINY ○ WINDY ○ FOGGY ○ COLD			
BUG NAME:					
WHERE DID YOU FIND IT?					
WHAT COLOR(S) IS THE BUG?					
NUMBER OF LEGS?		DOES IT HAVE WINGS?	○ YES ○ NO ○ NOT SURE		
NUMBER OF LEGS?					
THE BUG IS...		○ BIG ○ SHINY ○ FAST ○ SCARY ○ LITTLE ○ SLOW ○ CUTE ○ ROUND ○ THIN			
DOES IT MAKE ANY SOUND?	○ YES ○ NO	WAS IT ALONE OR IN A GROUP?	○ ALONE ○ GROUP		

NOTES

PHOTO/DRAWING

BUG JOURNAL

DATE:		TIME:		SEASON:	○ SPRING ○ SUMMER ○ FALL ○ WINTER		
WEATHER CONDITIONS:		○ HOT ○ WARM ○ SUNNY ○ CLOUDY ○ RAINY ○ WINDY ○ FOGGY ○ COLD					
BUG NAME:							
WHERE DID YOU FIND IT?							
WHAT COLOR(S) IS THE BUG?							
NUMBER OF LEGS?			DOES IT HAVE WINGS?	○ YES ○ NO ○ NOT SURE			
NUMBER OF LEGS?							
THE BUG IS...		○ BIG ○ SHINY ○ FAST ○ SCARY ○ LITTLE ○ SLOW ○ CUTE ○ ROUND ○ THIN					
DOES IT MAKE ANY SOUND?		○ YES ○ NO	WAS IT ALONE OR IN A GROUP?		○ ALONE ○ GROUP		

NOTES

PHOTO/DRAWING

BUG JOURNAL

DATE:		TIME:		SEASON:	○ SPRING ○ SUMMER ○ FALL ○ WINTER		
WEATHER CONDITIONS:		○ HOT ○ WARM ○ SUNNY ○ CLOUDY ○ RAINY ○ WINDY ○ FOGGY ○ COLD					
BUG NAME:							
WHERE DID YOU FIND IT?							
WHAT COLOR(S) IS THE BUG?							
NUMBER OF LEGS?		DOES IT HAVE WINGS?	○ YES ○ NO ○ NOT SURE				
NUMBER OF LEGS?							
THE BUG IS...		○ BIG ○ SHINY ○ FAST ○ SCARY ○ LITTLE ○ SLOW ○ CUTE ○ ROUND ○ THIN					
DOES IT MAKE ANY SOUND?	○ YES ○ NO	WAS IT ALONE OR IN A GROUP?	○ ALONE ○ GROUP				

NOTES

PHOTO/DRAWING

BUG JOURNAL

DATE:		TIME:		SEASON:	○ SPRING ○ SUMMER ○ FALL ○ WINTER
WEATHER CONDITIONS:		○ HOT ○ WARM ○ SUNNY ○ CLOUDY ○ RAINY ○ WINDY ○ FOGGY ○ COLD
BUG NAME:		
WHERE DID YOU FIND IT?		
WHAT COLOR(S) IS THE BUG?		
NUMBER OF LEGS?		DOES IT HAVE WINGS?	○ YES ○ NO ○ NOT SURE
NUMBER OF LEGS?		
THE BUG IS...		○ BIG ○ SHINY ○ FAST ○ SCARY ○ LITTLE ○ SLOW ○ CUTE ○ ROUND ○ THIN
DOES IT MAKE ANY SOUND?	○ YES ○ NO	WAS IT ALONE OR IN A GROUP?	○ ALONE ○ GROUP

NOTES

PHOTO/DRAWING

BUG JOURNAL

DATE:		TIME:		SEASON:	○ SPRING ○ SUMMER ○ FALL ○ WINTER
WEATHER CONDITIONS:		○ HOT ○ WARM ○ SUNNY ○ CLOUDY ○ RAINY ○ WINDY ○ FOGGY ○ COLD			
BUG NAME:					
WHERE DID YOU FIND IT?					
WHAT COLOR(S) IS THE BUG?					
NUMBER OF LEGS?		DOES IT HAVE WINGS?	○ YES ○ NO ○ NOT SURE		
NUMBER OF LEGS?					
THE BUG IS...		○ BIG ○ SHINY ○ FAST ○ SCARY ○ LITTLE ○ SLOW ○ CUTE ○ ROUND ○ THIN			
DOES IT MAKE ANY SOUND?	○ YES ○ NO	WAS IT ALONE OR IN A GROUP?	○ ALONE ○ GROUP		

NOTES

PHOTO/DRAWING

BUG JOURNAL

DATE:		TIME:		SEASON:	○ SPRING ○ SUMMER ○ FALL ○ WINTER		
WEATHER CONDITIONS:		○ HOT ○ WARM ○ SUNNY ○ CLOUDY ○ RAINY ○ WINDY ○ FOGGY ○ COLD					
BUG NAME:							
WHERE DID YOU FIND IT?							
WHAT COLOR(S) IS THE BUG?							
NUMBER OF LEGS?			DOES IT HAVE WINGS?	○ YES ○ NO ○ NOT SURE			
NUMBER OF LEGS?							
THE BUG IS...		○ BIG ○ SHINY ○ FAST ○ SCARY ○ LITTLE ○ SLOW ○ CUTE ○ ROUND ○ THIN					
DOES IT MAKE ANY SOUND?		○ YES ○ NO	WAS IT ALONE OR IN A GROUP?		○ ALONE ○ GROUP		

NOTES

PHOTO/DRAWING

BUG JOURNAL

DATE:		TIME:		SEASON:	○ SPRING ○ SUMMER ○ FALL ○ WINTER		
WEATHER CONDITIONS:		○ HOT ○ WARM ○ SUNNY ○ CLOUDY ○ RAINY ○ WINDY ○ FOGGY ○ COLD					
BUG NAME:							
WHERE DID YOU FIND IT?							
WHAT COLOR(S) IS THE BUG?							
NUMBER OF LEGS?			**DOES IT HAVE WINGS?**	○ YES ○ NO ○ NOT SURE			
NUMBER OF LEGS?							
THE BUG IS...		○ BIG ○ SHINY ○ FAST ○ SCARY ○ LITTLE ○ SLOW ○ CUTE ○ ROUND ○ THIN					
DOES IT MAKE ANY SOUND?	○ YES ○ NO	**WAS IT ALONE OR IN A GROUP?**	○ ALONE ○ GROUP				

NOTES

PHOTO/DRAWING

BUG JOURNAL

DATE:		TIME:		SEASON:	○ SPRING ○ SUMMER ○ FALL ○ WINTER

WEATHER CONDITIONS:	○ HOT ○ WARM ○ SUNNY ○ CLOUDY ○ RAINY ○ WINDY ○ FOGGY ○ COLD
BUG NAME:	
WHERE DID YOU FIND IT?	
WHAT COLOR(S) IS THE BUG?	

NUMBER OF LEGS?		DOES IT HAVE WINGS?	○ YES ○ NO ○ NOT SURE

NUMBER OF LEGS?	
THE BUG IS...	○ BIG ○ SHINY ○ FAST ○ SCARY ○ LITTLE ○ SLOW ○ CUTE ○ ROUND ○ THIN

DOES IT MAKE ANY SOUND?	○ YES ○ NO	WAS IT ALONE OR IN A GROUP?	○ ALONE ○ GROUP

NOTES

PHOTO/DRAWING

BUG JOURNAL

DATE:		TIME:		SEASON:	○ SPRING ○ SUMMER ○ FALL ○ WINTER

WEATHER CONDITIONS:	○ HOT ○ WARM ○ SUNNY ○ CLOUDY ○ RAINY ○ WINDY ○ FOGGY ○ COLD

BUG NAME:	
WHERE DID YOU FIND IT?	
WHAT COLOR(S) IS THE BUG?	

NUMBER OF LEGS?		DOES IT HAVE WINGS?	○ YES ○ NO ○ NOT SURE

NUMBER OF LEGS?	

THE BUG IS...	○ BIG ○ SHINY ○ FAST ○ SCARY ○ LITTLE ○ SLOW ○ CUTE ○ ROUND ○ THIN

DOES IT MAKE ANY SOUND?	○ YES ○ NO	WAS IT ALONE OR IN A GROUP?	○ ALONE ○ GROUP

NOTES

PHOTO/DRAWING

BUG JOURNAL

DATE:		TIME:		SEASON:	○ SPRING ○ SUMMER ○ FALL ○ WINTER
WEATHER CONDITIONS:		○ HOT ○ WARM ○ SUNNY ○ CLOUDY ○ RAINY ○ WINDY ○ FOGGY ○ COLD			
BUG NAME:					
WHERE DID YOU FIND IT?					
WHAT COLOR(S) IS THE BUG?					
NUMBER OF LEGS?		**DOES IT HAVE WINGS?**	○ YES ○ NO ○ NOT SURE		
NUMBER OF LEGS?					
THE BUG IS...		○ BIG ○ SHINY ○ FAST ○ SCARY ○ LITTLE ○ SLOW ○ CUTE ○ ROUND ○ THIN			
DOES IT MAKE ANY SOUND?	○ YES ○ NO	**WAS IT ALONE OR IN A GROUP?**	○ ALONE ○ GROUP		

NOTES

PHOTO/DRAWING

BUG JOURNAL

DATE:		TIME:		SEASON:	○ SPRING ○ SUMMER ○ FALL ○ WINTER
WEATHER CONDITIONS:		○ HOT ○ WARM ○ SUNNY ○ CLOUDY ○ RAINY ○ WINDY ○ FOGGY ○ COLD			
BUG NAME:					
WHERE DID YOU FIND IT?					
WHAT COLOR(S) IS THE BUG?					
NUMBER OF LEGS?		**DOES IT HAVE WINGS?**	○ YES ○ NO ○ NOT SURE		
NUMBER OF LEGS?					
THE BUG IS...		○ BIG ○ SHINY ○ FAST ○ SCARY ○ LITTLE ○ SLOW ○ CUTE ○ ROUND ○ THIN			
DOES IT MAKE ANY SOUND?	○ YES ○ NO	**WAS IT ALONE OR IN A GROUP?**	○ ALONE ○ GROUP		

NOTES

PHOTO/DRAWING

BUG JOURNAL

DATE:		TIME:		SEASON:	○ SPRING ○ SUMMER ○ FALL ○ WINTER		
WEATHER CONDITIONS:		○ HOT ○ WARM ○ SUNNY ○ CLOUDY ○ RAINY ○ WINDY ○ FOGGY ○ COLD					
BUG NAME:							
WHERE DID YOU FIND IT?							
WHAT COLOR(S) IS THE BUG?							
NUMBER OF LEGS?			DOES IT HAVE WINGS?	○ YES ○ NO ○ NOT SURE			
NUMBER OF LEGS?							
THE BUG IS...		○ BIG ○ SHINY ○ FAST ○ SCARY ○ LITTLE ○ SLOW ○ CUTE ○ ROUND ○ THIN					
DOES IT MAKE ANY SOUND?	○ YES ○ NO	WAS IT ALONE OR IN A GROUP?		○ ALONE ○ GROUP			

NOTES

PHOTO/DRAWING

BUG JOURNAL

DATE:		TIME:		SEASON:	○ SPRING ○ SUMMER ○ FALL ○ WINTER

WEATHER CONDITIONS:	○ HOT ○ WARM ○ SUNNY ○ CLOUDY ○ RAINY ○ WINDY ○ FOGGY ○ COLD
BUG NAME:	
WHERE DID YOU FIND IT?	
WHAT COLOR(S) IS THE BUG?	

NUMBER OF LEGS?		DOES IT HAVE WINGS?	○ YES ○ NO ○ NOT SURE

NUMBER OF LEGS?	
THE BUG IS...	○ BIG ○ SHINY ○ FAST ○ SCARY ○ LITTLE ○ SLOW ○ CUTE ○ ROUND ○ THIN

DOES IT MAKE ANY SOUND?	○ YES ○ NO	WAS IT ALONE OR IN A GROUP?	○ ALONE ○ GROUP

NOTES

PHOTO/DRAWING

BUG JOURNAL

DATE:		TIME:		SEASON:	○ SPRING ○ SUMMER ○ FALL ○ WINTER
WEATHER CONDITIONS:					○ HOT ○ WARM ○ SUNNY ○ CLOUDY ○ RAINY ○ WINDY ○ FOGGY ○ COLD
BUG NAME:					
WHERE DID YOU FIND IT?					
WHAT COLOR(S) IS THE BUG?					
NUMBER OF LEGS?			**DOES IT HAVE WINGS?**	○ YES ○ NO ○ NOT SURE	
NUMBER OF LEGS?					
THE BUG IS...		○ BIG ○ SHINY ○ FAST ○ SCARY ○ LITTLE ○ SLOW ○ CUTE ○ ROUND ○ THIN			
DOES IT MAKE ANY SOUND?	○ YES ○ NO	**WAS IT ALONE OR IN A GROUP?**		○ ALONE ○ GROUP	

NOTES

PHOTO/DRAWING

BUG JOURNAL

DATE:		TIME:		SEASON:	○ SPRING ○ SUMMER ○ FALL ○ WINTER
WEATHER CONDITIONS:				○ HOT ○ WARM ○ SUNNY ○ CLOUDY ○ RAINY ○ WINDY ○ FOGGY ○ COLD	
BUG NAME:					
WHERE DID YOU FIND IT?					
WHAT COLOR(S) IS THE BUG?					
NUMBER OF LEGS?		**DOES IT HAVE WINGS?**	○ YES ○ NO ○ NOT SURE		
NUMBER OF LEGS?					
THE BUG IS...		○ BIG ○ SHINY ○ FAST ○ SCARY ○ LITTLE ○ SLOW ○ CUTE ○ ROUND ○ THIN			
DOES IT MAKE ANY SOUND?	○ YES ○ NO	**WAS IT ALONE OR IN A GROUP?**	○ ALONE ○ GROUP		

NOTES

PHOTO/DRAWING

BUG JOURNAL

DATE:		TIME:		SEASON:	○ SPRING ○ SUMMER ○ FALL ○ WINTER		
WEATHER CONDITIONS:		○ HOT ○ WARM ○ SUNNY ○ CLOUDY ○ RAINY ○ WINDY ○ FOGGY ○ COLD					
BUG NAME:							
WHERE DID YOU FIND IT?							
WHAT COLOR(S) IS THE BUG?							
NUMBER OF LEGS?			DOES IT HAVE WINGS?	○ YES ○ NO ○ NOT SURE			
NUMBER OF LEGS?							
THE BUG IS...		○ BIG ○ SHINY ○ FAST ○ SCARY ○ LITTLE ○ SLOW ○ CUTE ○ ROUND ○ THIN					
DOES IT MAKE ANY SOUND?	○ YES ○ NO		WAS IT ALONE OR IN A GROUP?		○ ALONE ○ GROUP		

NOTES

PHOTO/DRAWING

BUG JOURNAL

DATE:		TIME:		SEASON:	○ SPRING ○ SUMMER ○ FALL ○ WINTER
WEATHER CONDITIONS:		○ HOT ○ WARM ○ SUNNY ○ CLOUDY ○ RAINY ○ WINDY ○ FOGGY ○ COLD			
BUG NAME:					
WHERE DID YOU FIND IT?					
WHAT COLOR(S) IS THE BUG?					
NUMBER OF LEGS?		**DOES IT HAVE WINGS?**	○ YES ○ NO ○ NOT SURE		
NUMBER OF LEGS?					
THE BUG IS...		○ BIG ○ SHINY ○ FAST ○ SCARY ○ LITTLE ○ SLOW ○ CUTE ○ ROUND ○ THIN			
DOES IT MAKE ANY SOUND?	○ YES ○ NO	**WAS IT ALONE OR IN A GROUP?**	○ ALONE ○ GROUP		

NOTES

PHOTO/DRAWING

BUG JOURNAL

DATE:		TIME:		SEASON:	○ SPRING ○ SUMMER ○ FALL ○ WINTER
WEATHER CONDITIONS:		○ HOT ○ WARM ○ SUNNY ○ CLOUDY ○ RAINY ○ WINDY ○ FOGGY ○ COLD				
BUG NAME:						
WHERE DID YOU FIND IT?						
WHAT COLOR(S) IS THE BUG?						
NUMBER OF LEGS?		DOES IT HAVE WINGS?	○ YES ○ NO ○ NOT SURE			
NUMBER OF LEGS?						
THE BUG IS...	○ BIG ○ SHINY ○ FAST ○ SCARY ○ LITTLE ○ SLOW ○ CUTE ○ ROUND ○ THIN				
DOES IT MAKE ANY SOUND?	○ YES ○ NO	WAS IT ALONE OR IN A GROUP?	○ ALONE ○ GROUP			

NOTES

PHOTO/DRAWING

BUG JOURNAL

DATE:		TIME:		SEASON:	○ SPRING ○ SUMMER ○ FALL ○ WINTER
WEATHER CONDITIONS:			○ HOT ○ WARM ○ SUNNY ○ CLOUDY ○ RAINY ○ WINDY ○ FOGGY ○ COLD		
BUG NAME:					
WHERE DID YOU FIND IT?					
WHAT COLOR(S) IS THE BUG?					
NUMBER OF LEGS?		DOES IT HAVE WINGS?	○ YES ○ NO ○ NOT SURE		
NUMBER OF LEGS?					
THE BUG IS...			○ BIG ○ SHINY ○ FAST ○ SCARY ○ LITTLE ○ SLOW ○ CUTE ○ ROUND ○ THIN		
DOES IT MAKE ANY SOUND?	○ YES ○ NO	WAS IT ALONE OR IN A GROUP?	○ ALONE ○ GROUP		

NOTES

PHOTO/DRAWING

BUG JOURNAL

DATE:		TIME:		SEASON:	○ SPRING ○ SUMMER ○ FALL ○ WINTER		
WEATHER CONDITIONS:		○ HOT ○ WARM ○ SUNNY ○ CLOUDY ○ RAINY ○ WINDY ○ FOGGY ○ COLD					
BUG NAME:							
WHERE DID YOU FIND IT?							
WHAT COLOR(S) IS THE BUG?							
NUMBER OF LEGS?		DOES IT HAVE WINGS?	○ YES ○ NO ○ NOT SURE				
NUMBER OF LEGS?							
THE BUG IS...		○ BIG ○ SHINY ○ FAST ○ SCARY ○ LITTLE ○ SLOW ○ CUTE ○ ROUND ○ THIN					
DOES IT MAKE ANY SOUND?	○ YES ○ NO	WAS IT ALONE OR IN A GROUP?	○ ALONE ○ GROUP				

NOTES

PHOTO/DRAWING

BUG JOURNAL

DATE:		TIME:		SEASON:	○ SPRING ○ SUMMER ○ FALL ○ WINTER
WEATHER CONDITIONS:			○ HOT ○ WARM ○ SUNNY ○ CLOUDY ○ RAINY ○ WINDY ○ FOGGY ○ COLD		
BUG NAME:					
WHERE DID YOU FIND IT?					
WHAT COLOR(S) IS THE BUG?					
NUMBER OF LEGS?		DOES IT HAVE WINGS?	○ YES ○ NO ○ NOT SURE		
NUMBER OF LEGS?					
THE BUG IS...		○ BIG ○ SHINY ○ FAST ○ SCARY ○ LITTLE ○ SLOW ○ CUTE ○ ROUND ○ THIN			
DOES IT MAKE ANY SOUND?	○ YES ○ NO	WAS IT ALONE OR IN A GROUP?	○ ALONE ○ GROUP		

NOTES

PHOTO/DRAWING

BUG JOURNAL

DATE:		TIME:		SEASON:	○ SPRING ○ SUMMER ○ FALL ○ WINTER
WEATHER CONDITIONS:		○ HOT ○ WARM ○ SUNNY ○ CLOUDY ○ RAINY ○ WINDY ○ FOGGY ○ COLD			
BUG NAME:					
WHERE DID YOU FIND IT?					
WHAT COLOR(S) IS THE BUG?					
NUMBER OF LEGS?		DOES IT HAVE WINGS?	○ YES ○ NO ○ NOT SURE		
NUMBER OF LEGS?					
THE BUG IS...		○ BIG ○ SHINY ○ FAST ○ SCARY ○ LITTLE ○ SLOW ○ CUTE ○ ROUND ○ THIN			
DOES IT MAKE ANY SOUND?	○ YES ○ NO	WAS IT ALONE OR IN A GROUP?	○ ALONE ○ GROUP		

NOTES

PHOTO/DRAWING

BUG JOURNAL

DATE:		TIME:		SEASON:	○ SPRING ○ SUMMER ○ FALL ○ WINTER

WEATHER CONDITIONS:	○ HOT ○ WARM ○ SUNNY ○ CLOUDY ○ RAINY ○ WINDY ○ FOGGY ○ COLD
BUG NAME:	
WHERE DID YOU FIND IT?	
WHAT COLOR(S) IS THE BUG?	

NUMBER OF LEGS?		DOES IT HAVE WINGS?	○ YES ○ NO ○ NOT SURE

NUMBER OF LEGS?	
THE BUG IS...	○ BIG ○ SHINY ○ FAST ○ SCARY ○ LITTLE ○ SLOW ○ CUTE ○ ROUND ○ THIN

DOES IT MAKE ANY SOUND?	○ YES ○ NO	WAS IT ALONE OR IN A GROUP?	○ ALONE ○ GROUP

NOTES

PHOTO/DRAWING

BUG JOURNAL

DATE:		TIME:		SEASON:	○ SPRING ○ SUMMER ○ FALL ○ WINTER		
WEATHER CONDITIONS:		○ HOT ○ WARM ○ SUNNY ○ CLOUDY ○ RAINY ○ WINDY ○ FOGGY ○ COLD					
BUG NAME:							
WHERE DID YOU FIND IT?							
WHAT COLOR(S) IS THE BUG?							
NUMBER OF LEGS?			DOES IT HAVE WINGS?	○ YES ○ NO ○ NOT SURE			
NUMBER OF LEGS?							
THE BUG IS...		○ BIG ○ SHINY ○ FAST ○ SCARY ○ LITTLE ○ SLOW ○ CUTE ○ ROUND ○ THIN					
DOES IT MAKE ANY SOUND?	○ YES ○ NO	WAS IT ALONE OR IN A GROUP?		○ ALONE ○ GROUP			

NOTES

PHOTO/DRAWING

BUG JOURNAL

DATE:		TIME:		SEASON:	○ SPRING ○ SUMMER ○ FALL ○ WINTER
WEATHER CONDITIONS:		○ HOT ○ WARM ○ SUNNY ○ CLOUDY ○ RAINY ○ WINDY ○ FOGGY ○ COLD			
BUG NAME:					
WHERE DID YOU FIND IT?					
WHAT COLOR(S) IS THE BUG?					
NUMBER OF LEGS?		DOES IT HAVE WINGS?	○ YES ○ NO ○ NOT SURE		
NUMBER OF LEGS?					
THE BUG IS...		○ BIG ○ SHINY ○ FAST ○ SCARY ○ LITTLE ○ SLOW ○ CUTE ○ ROUND ○ THIN			
DOES IT MAKE ANY SOUND?	○ YES ○ NO	WAS IT ALONE OR IN A GROUP?	○ ALONE ○ GROUP		

NOTES

PHOTO/DRAWING

BUG JOURNAL

DATE:		TIME:		SEASON:	○ SPRING ○ SUMMER ○ FALL ○ WINTER
WEATHER CONDITIONS:		○ HOT ○ WARM ○ SUNNY ○ CLOUDY ○ RAINY ○ WINDY ○ FOGGY ○ COLD			
BUG NAME:					
WHERE DID YOU FIND IT?					
WHAT COLOR(S) IS THE BUG?					
NUMBER OF LEGS?		DOES IT HAVE WINGS?	○ YES ○ NO ○ NOT SURE		
NUMBER OF LEGS?					
THE BUG IS...		○ BIG ○ SHINY ○ FAST ○ SCARY ○ LITTLE ○ SLOW ○ CUTE ○ ROUND ○ THIN			
DOES IT MAKE ANY SOUND?	○ YES ○ NO	WAS IT ALONE OR IN A GROUP?	○ ALONE ○ GROUP		

NOTES

PHOTO/DRAWING

BUG JOURNAL

DATE:		TIME:		SEASON:	○ SPRING ○ SUMMER ○ FALL ○ WINTER
WEATHER CONDITIONS:					○ HOT ○ WARM ○ SUNNY ○ CLOUDY ○ RAINY ○ WINDY ○ FOGGY ○ COLD
BUG NAME:					
WHERE DID YOU FIND IT?					
WHAT COLOR(S) IS THE BUG?					
NUMBER OF LEGS?		**DOES IT HAVE WINGS?**			○ YES ○ NO ○ NOT SURE
NUMBER OF LEGS?					
THE BUG IS...					○ BIG ○ SHINY ○ FAST ○ SCARY ○ LITTLE ○ SLOW ○ CUTE ○ ROUND ○ THIN
DOES IT MAKE ANY SOUND?	○ YES ○ NO	**WAS IT ALONE OR IN A GROUP?**			○ ALONE ○ GROUP

NOTES

PHOTO/DRAWING

BUG JOURNAL

DATE:		TIME:		SEASON:	○ SPRING ○ SUMMER ○ FALL ○ WINTER
WEATHER CONDITIONS:			○ HOT ○ WARM ○ SUNNY ○ CLOUDY ○ RAINY ○ WINDY ○ FOGGY ○ COLD		
BUG NAME:					
WHERE DID YOU FIND IT?					
WHAT COLOR(S) IS THE BUG?					
NUMBER OF LEGS?			**DOES IT HAVE WINGS?**	○ YES ○ NO ○ NOT SURE	
NUMBER OF LEGS?					
THE BUG IS...			○ BIG ○ SHINY ○ FAST ○ SCARY ○ LITTLE ○ SLOW ○ CUTE ○ ROUND ○ THIN		
DOES IT MAKE ANY SOUND?	○ YES ○ NO	**WAS IT ALONE OR IN A GROUP?**	○ ALONE ○ GROUP		

NOTES

PHOTO/DRAWING

BUG JOURNAL

DATE:		TIME:		SEASON:	○ SPRING ○ SUMMER ○ FALL ○ WINTER
WEATHER CONDITIONS:		○ HOT ○ WARM ○ SUNNY ○ CLOUDY ○ RAINY ○ WINDY ○ FOGGY ○ COLD			
BUG NAME:					
WHERE DID YOU FIND IT?					
WHAT COLOR(S) IS THE BUG?					
NUMBER OF LEGS?		DOES IT HAVE WINGS?	○ YES ○ NO ○ NOT SURE		
NUMBER OF LEGS?					
THE BUG IS...	○ BIG ○ SHINY ○ FAST ○ SCARY ○ LITTLE ○ SLOW ○ CUTE ○ ROUND ○ THIN				
DOES IT MAKE ANY SOUND?	○ YES ○ NO	WAS IT ALONE OR IN A GROUP?	○ ALONE ○ GROUP		

NOTES

PHOTO/DRAWING

BUG JOURNAL

DATE:		TIME:		SEASON:	○ SPRING ○ SUMMER ○ FALL ○ WINTER		
WEATHER CONDITIONS:		○ HOT ○ WARM ○ SUNNY ○ CLOUDY ○ RAINY ○ WINDY ○ FOGGY ○ COLD					
BUG NAME:							
WHERE DID YOU FIND IT?							
WHAT COLOR(S) IS THE BUG?							
NUMBER OF LEGS?		DOES IT HAVE WINGS?	○ YES ○ NO ○ NOT SURE				
NUMBER OF LEGS?							
THE BUG IS...		○ BIG ○ SHINY ○ FAST ○ SCARY ○ LITTLE ○ SLOW ○ CUTE ○ ROUND ○ THIN					
DOES IT MAKE ANY SOUND?	○ YES ○ NO	WAS IT ALONE OR IN A GROUP?	○ ALONE ○ GROUP				

NOTES

PHOTO/DRAWING

BUG JOURNAL

DATE:		TIME:		SEASON:	○ SPRING ○ SUMMER ○ FALL ○ WINTER
WEATHER CONDITIONS:			○ HOT ○ WARM ○ SUNNY ○ CLOUDY ○ RAINY ○ WINDY ○ FOGGY ○ COLD
BUG NAME:			
WHERE DID YOU FIND IT?			
WHAT COLOR(S) IS THE BUG?			
NUMBER OF LEGS?		DOES IT HAVE WINGS?	○ YES ○ NO ○ NOT SURE
NUMBER OF LEGS?			
THE BUG IS...		○ BIG ○ SHINY ○ FAST ○ SCARY ○ LITTLE ○ SLOW ○ CUTE ○ ROUND ○ THIN
DOES IT MAKE ANY SOUND?	○ YES ○ NO	WAS IT ALONE OR IN A GROUP?	○ ALONE ○ GROUP

NOTES

PHOTO/DRAWING

BUG JOURNAL

DATE:		TIME:		SEASON:	○ SPRING ○ SUMMER ○ FALL ○ WINTER
WEATHER CONDITIONS:		○ HOT ○ WARM ○ SUNNY ○ CLOUDY ○ RAINY ○ WINDY ○ FOGGY ○ COLD			
BUG NAME:					
WHERE DID YOU FIND IT?					
WHAT COLOR(S) IS THE BUG?					
NUMBER OF LEGS?		DOES IT HAVE WINGS?	○ YES ○ NO ○ NOT SURE		
NUMBER OF LEGS?					
THE BUG IS...		○ BIG ○ SHINY ○ FAST ○ SCARY ○ LITTLE ○ SLOW ○ CUTE ○ ROUND ○ THIN			
DOES IT MAKE ANY SOUND?	○ YES ○ NO	WAS IT ALONE OR IN A GROUP?	○ ALONE ○ GROUP		

NOTES

PHOTO/DRAWING

BUG JOURNAL

DATE:		TIME:		SEASON:	○ SPRING ○ SUMMER ○ FALL ○ WINTER
WEATHER CONDITIONS:		○ HOT ○ WARM ○ SUNNY ○ CLOUDY ○ RAINY ○ WINDY ○ FOGGY ○ COLD			
BUG NAME:					
WHERE DID YOU FIND IT?					
WHAT COLOR(S) IS THE BUG?					
NUMBER OF LEGS?		**DOES IT HAVE WINGS?**	○ YES ○ NO ○ NOT SURE		
NUMBER OF LEGS?					
THE BUG IS...		○ BIG ○ SHINY ○ FAST ○ SCARY ○ LITTLE ○ SLOW ○ CUTE ○ ROUND ○ THIN			
DOES IT MAKE ANY SOUND?	○ YES ○ NO	**WAS IT ALONE OR IN A GROUP?**	○ ALONE ○ GROUP		

NOTES

PHOTO/DRAWING

BUG JOURNAL

DATE:		TIME:		SEASON:	○ SPRING ○ SUMMER ○ FALL ○ WINTER		
WEATHER CONDITIONS:		○ HOT ○ WARM ○ SUNNY ○ CLOUDY ○ RAINY ○ WINDY ○ FOGGY ○ COLD					
BUG NAME:							
WHERE DID YOU FIND IT?							
WHAT COLOR(S) IS THE BUG?							
NUMBER OF LEGS?			DOES IT HAVE WINGS?	○ YES ○ NO ○ NOT SURE			
NUMBER OF LEGS?							
THE BUG IS...		○ BIG ○ SHINY ○ FAST ○ SCARY ○ LITTLE ○ SLOW ○ CUTE ○ ROUND ○ THIN					
DOES IT MAKE ANY SOUND?	○ YES ○ NO		WAS IT ALONE OR IN A GROUP?		○ ALONE ○ GROUP		

NOTES

PHOTO/DRAWING

BUG JOURNAL

DATE:		TIME:		SEASON:	○ SPRING ○ SUMMER ○ FALL ○ WINTER

WEATHER CONDITIONS:	○ HOT ○ WARM ○ SUNNY ○ CLOUDY ○ RAINY ○ WINDY ○ FOGGY ○ COLD
BUG NAME:	
WHERE DID YOU FIND IT?	
WHAT COLOR(S) IS THE BUG?	

NUMBER OF LEGS?		DOES IT HAVE WINGS?	○ YES ○ NO ○ NOT SURE

NUMBER OF LEGS?	
THE BUG IS...	○ BIG ○ SHINY ○ FAST ○ SCARY ○ LITTLE ○ SLOW ○ CUTE ○ ROUND ○ THIN

DOES IT MAKE ANY SOUND?	○ YES ○ NO	WAS IT ALONE OR IN A GROUP?	○ ALONE ○ GROUP

NOTES

PHOTO/DRAWING

BUG JOURNAL

DATE:		TIME:		SEASON:	○ SPRING ○ SUMMER ○ FALL ○ WINTER		
WEATHER CONDITIONS:		○ HOT ○ WARM ○ SUNNY ○ CLOUDY ○ RAINY ○ WINDY ○ FOGGY ○ COLD					
BUG NAME:							
WHERE DID YOU FIND IT?							
WHAT COLOR(S) IS THE BUG?							
NUMBER OF LEGS?		**DOES IT HAVE WINGS?**	○ YES ○ NO ○ NOT SURE				
NUMBER OF LEGS?							
THE BUG IS...		○ BIG ○ SHINY ○ FAST ○ SCARY ○ LITTLE ○ SLOW ○ CUTE ○ ROUND ○ THIN					
DOES IT MAKE ANY SOUND?	○ YES ○ NO	**WAS IT ALONE OR IN A GROUP?**	○ ALONE ○ GROUP				

NOTES

PHOTO/DRAWING

BUG JOURNAL

DATE:		TIME:		SEASON:	○ SPRING ○ SUMMER ○ FALL ○ WINTER

WEATHER CONDITIONS:	○ HOT ○ WARM ○ SUNNY ○ CLOUDY ○ RAINY ○ WINDY ○ FOGGY ○ COLD

BUG NAME:	
WHERE DID YOU FIND IT?	
WHAT COLOR(S) IS THE BUG?	

NUMBER OF LEGS?		DOES IT HAVE WINGS?	○ YES ○ NO ○ NOT SURE

NUMBER OF LEGS?	

THE BUG IS...	○ BIG ○ SHINY ○ FAST ○ SCARY ○ LITTLE ○ SLOW ○ CUTE ○ ROUND ○ THIN

DOES IT MAKE ANY SOUND?	○ YES ○ NO	WAS IT ALONE OR IN A GROUP?	○ ALONE ○ GROUP

NOTES

PHOTO/DRAWING

BUG JOURNAL

DATE:		TIME:		SEASON:	○ SPRING ○ SUMMER ○ FALL ○ WINTER

WEATHER CONDITIONS:	○ HOT ○ WARM ○ SUNNY ○ CLOUDY ○ RAINY ○ WINDY ○ FOGGY ○ COLD
BUG NAME:	
WHERE DID YOU FIND IT?	
WHAT COLOR(S) IS THE BUG?	

NUMBER OF LEGS?		DOES IT HAVE WINGS?	○ YES ○ NO ○ NOT SURE

NUMBER OF LEGS?	
THE BUG IS...	○ BIG ○ SHINY ○ FAST ○ SCARY ○ LITTLE ○ SLOW ○ CUTE ○ ROUND ○ THIN

DOES IT MAKE ANY SOUND?	○ YES ○ NO	WAS IT ALONE OR IN A GROUP?	○ ALONE ○ GROUP

NOTES

PHOTO/DRAWING

BUG JOURNAL

DATE:		TIME:		SEASON:	○ SPRING ○ SUMMER ○ FALL ○ WINTER

WEATHER CONDITIONS:	○ HOT ○ WARM ○ SUNNY ○ CLOUDY ○ RAINY ○ WINDY ○ FOGGY ○ COLD
BUG NAME:	
WHERE DID YOU FIND IT?	
WHAT COLOR(S) IS THE BUG?	

NUMBER OF LEGS?		DOES IT HAVE WINGS?	○ YES ○ NO ○ NOT SURE

NUMBER OF LEGS?	
THE BUG IS...	○ BIG ○ SHINY ○ FAST ○ SCARY ○ LITTLE ○ SLOW ○ CUTE ○ ROUND ○ THIN

DOES IT MAKE ANY SOUND?	○ YES ○ NO	WAS IT ALONE OR IN A GROUP?	○ ALONE ○ GROUP

NOTES

PHOTO/DRAWING

BUG JOURNAL

DATE:		TIME:		SEASON:	○ SPRING ○ SUMMER ○ FALL ○ WINTER
WEATHER CONDITIONS:		○ HOT ○ WARM ○ SUNNY ○ CLOUDY ○ RAINY ○ WINDY ○ FOGGY ○ COLD			
BUG NAME:					
WHERE DID YOU FIND IT?					
WHAT COLOR(S) IS THE BUG?					
NUMBER OF LEGS?		**DOES IT HAVE WINGS?**	○ YES ○ NO ○ NOT SURE		
NUMBER OF LEGS?					
THE BUG IS...		○ BIG ○ SHINY ○ FAST ○ SCARY ○ LITTLE ○ SLOW ○ CUTE ○ ROUND ○ THIN			
DOES IT MAKE ANY SOUND?	○ YES ○ NO	**WAS IT ALONE OR IN A GROUP?**	○ ALONE ○ GROUP		

NOTES

PHOTO/DRAWING

BUG JOURNAL

DATE:		TIME:		SEASON:	○ SPRING ○ SUMMER ○ FALL ○ WINTER
WEATHER CONDITIONS:					○ HOT ○ WARM ○ SUNNY ○ CLOUDY ○ RAINY ○ WINDY ○ FOGGY ○ COLD
BUG NAME:					
WHERE DID YOU FIND IT?					
WHAT COLOR(S) IS THE BUG?					
NUMBER OF LEGS?			DOES IT HAVE WINGS?	○ YES ○ NO ○ NOT SURE	
NUMBER OF LEGS?					
THE BUG IS...		○ BIG ○ SHINY ○ FAST ○ SCARY ○ LITTLE ○ SLOW ○ CUTE ○ ROUND ○ THIN			
DOES IT MAKE ANY SOUND?	○ YES ○ NO	WAS IT ALONE OR IN A GROUP?	○ ALONE ○ GROUP		

NOTES

PHOTO/DRAWING

BUG JOURNAL

DATE:			TIME:		SEASON:	○ SPRING ○ SUMMER ○ FALL ○ WINTER
WEATHER CONDITIONS:			○ HOT ○ WARM ○ SUNNY ○ CLOUDY ○ RAINY ○ WINDY ○ FOGGY ○ COLD
BUG NAME:			
WHERE DID YOU FIND IT?			
WHAT COLOR(S) IS THE BUG?			
NUMBER OF LEGS?		DOES IT HAVE WINGS?	○ YES ○ NO ○ NOT SURE
NUMBER OF LEGS?			
THE BUG IS...		○ BIG ○ SHINY ○ FAST ○ SCARY ○ LITTLE ○ SLOW ○ CUTE ○ ROUND ○ THIN
DOES IT MAKE ANY SOUND?	○ YES ○ NO	WAS IT ALONE OR IN A GROUP?	○ ALONE ○ GROUP

NOTES

PHOTO/DRAWING

BUG JOURNAL

DATE:		TIME:		SEASON:	○ SPRING ○ SUMMER ○ FALL ○ WINTER
WEATHER CONDITIONS:		○ HOT ○ WARM ○ SUNNY ○ CLOUDY ○ RAINY ○ WINDY ○ FOGGY ○ COLD			
BUG NAME:					
WHERE DID YOU FIND IT?					
WHAT COLOR(S) IS THE BUG?					
NUMBER OF LEGS?		**DOES IT HAVE WINGS?**	○ YES ○ NO ○ NOT SURE		
NUMBER OF LEGS?					
THE BUG IS...		○ BIG ○ SHINY ○ FAST ○ SCARY ○ LITTLE ○ SLOW ○ CUTE ○ ROUND ○ THIN			
DOES IT MAKE ANY SOUND?	○ YES ○ NO	**WAS IT ALONE OR IN A GROUP?**	○ ALONE ○ GROUP		

NOTES

PHOTO/DRAWING

www.ingramcontent.com/pod-product-compliance
Lightning Source LLC
Chambersburg PA
CBHW051033030426
42336CB00015B/2854